The Food Teacher
on UK Health Radio

The show about the importance of food to improve health and well being

Launching on Saturday 3rd September, with **'All about Gluten!'**

ukhealthradio.com
thefoodteacher.co.uk
Facebook: thefoodteacheruk
Twitter: foodteacheruk
Instagram: thefoodteacher

Health Radio
real "feel good" radio ...

Acknowledgements

The assistance of all the pilot schools in supporting the development of these materials is gratefully acknowledged.

Specific thanks to Manland Primary School, Attleborough Infant School, Harpenden Academy and Larwood School for their support and detailed feedback. Thank you also to all the children involved in the photography.

Special thanks to Katy Wilmshurst, Penny Bird and Camera, Luke Godward (design) and Sue Tate.

Above all an extra special thanks to Tim and Alice for all your help, support and taste testing.

Disclaimer

The author wishes to make it clear that they accept no responsibility for any liability, loss or risk, personal or otherwise, which is incurred as a result of using any of the recipes and/or recommendations suggested herein. It is the users responsibility to ensure that any information or ingredients are suitable for those who will consume them. If in any doubt, or if requiring medical advice, please contact the appropriate health professional.

First published in Great Britain by Katharine Tate, The Food Teacher in 2015.

Contents

© The Food Teacher

Introduction

Welcome to 'Heat-Free and Healthy'. This book illustrates how adults and children can create simple, nutritious food at home without using a cooker.

As The Food Teacher, I work with both children and adults in schools, within the community or at The Food Teacher clinic.

Many of these recipes were written for school use to enable schools without cookery facilities or access to kitchens to deliver the 'Cooking and Nutrition' curriculum within their classrooms. A companion book to this one, 'No Kitchen Cookery for Primary Schools' is available for schools. This aims to give teachers an outline for cookery lessons mapped to the 'Cooking and Nutrition' curriculum with objectives, outcomes and assessment opportunities clearly identified alongside Key Stage appropriate, easy to follow recipes.

Through my clinics and workshops I am frequently asked for recipe suggestions which are healthy, nutritious and quick to prepare. The 40 recipes within 'Heat-Free and Healthy' tick all those boxes. Given these recipes do not require heat, the time from start to table is relatively short with many being ready in under 15 minutes.

For parents using this book a list of key cookery skills have been included which outline the ages of skill development inline with the school curriculum. An equipment checklist and some top tips for food safety are also included.

Recipes focus on balancing blood sugar, most don't contain gluten and they also use a range of fruit and vegetables, which are all parameters for nutritious options that benefit our bodies.

Each recipe lists specific equipment needed and nutrition know how. Detailed nutrient information and a glossary of terms are found at the back.

Dietary adaptations have been included (**DF** - Dairy Free, **GF** - Gluten Free, **NF** - Nut Free) but please consider allergies and intolerances when preparing these recipes at home.

Recipes are grouped into 7 sections:
- Breakfasts
- Salads
- Sandwiches & Wraps
- Dips
- Snacks
- Desserts
- Drinks

Look out for forthcoming books, events and demonstrations within your community.

About the Author

The Food Teacher, Katharine Tate, has worked as a teacher and education consultant internationally in primary and secondary schools for over 20 years. Qualified as a registered nutritional therapist, Katharine combines her unique education and nutrition expertise to offer schools, organisations and families advice, education programmes, practical workshops, and individual/family consultations.

Katharine Tate, The Food Teacher
BEd (Hons), FAETC, Dip ION (Distinction), BANT, CNHC

Key Cookery Skills

Key skills mapped to development and suggested ages.

Knife Skills

Skill	Ingredients for skill practice	Recipe numbers	4+	5+	6+	7+	8+	9+	10+
Cutting food with scissors	Apricots, dates	17, 21, 23, 24, 58	●	●	●	●	●	●	●
Bridge knife techniques — soft foods	Strawberry, cherry tomato	17, 24, 27, 32, 33, 34, 52, 53, 58, 59, 60, 68, 69,	●	●	●	●	●	●	●
Bridge knife technique — harder foods	Apple	20, 24, 33, 34			●	●	●	●	●
Claw knife technique — soft foods	Cucumber	17, 24, 33, 34, 41, 43, 45, 51, 55		●	●	●	●	●	●
Claw knife technique — harder foods	Carrot	24, 33, 43, 50, 68			●	●	●	●	●
Simple combination of bridge and claw	Onion, orange	20, 21, 22, 24, 39, 67						●	●
Fine chopping of herbs	Chives, parsley, coriander	35, 39, 45							●
Snipping herbs in a jug using scissors	Chives, parsley, coriander	23, 39, 40, 43		●	●	●	●	●	●
Peeling soft vegetables	Courgette					●	●	●	●
Peeling harder vegetables	Carrot, potato	20, 35						●	●
Grating soft foods	Courgette, cheese	33, 58, 59, 60			●	●	●	●	●
Grating harder foods	Carrot, apple	20, 33					●	●	●

Skill	Ingredients for skill practice	Recipe numbers	4+	5+	6+	7+	8+	9+	10+
Finer grating	Parmesan cheese, nutmeg	59					●	●	●

Weighing and Measuring

Skill	Ingredients for skill practice	Recipe numbers	4+	5+	6+	7+	8+	9+	10+
Using measuring spoons and cups	Spices, herbs, oil	17, 20, 21, 22, 23, 26, 27, 38, 40, 41, 42, 43, 44, 52, 60, 67, 68	●	●	●	●	●	●	●
Using a jug to measure liquids	Juice, oil, milk	43, 67, 68, 69			●	●	●	●	●
Using balance scales	Beans, fish, yoghurt	21, 22, 23, 41	●	●	●	●	●	●	●
Counting out ingredients	Fruits, vegetables	55, 53, 22	●	●	●	●	●	●	●
Using digital or spring balance scales	Beans, fish, yoghurt	23, 21, 52, 41			●	●	●	●	●

Other

Skill	Ingredients for skill practice	Recipe numbers	4+	5+	6+	7+	8+	9	10+
Tearing	Herbs	23, 40	●	●	●	●	●	●	●
Crumbling cheese	Feta cheese	21, 40, 44	●	●	●	●	●	●	●
Arranging ingredients/toppings	Layered salad		●	●	●	●	●	●	●
Spreading with the back of a spoon	Pizza topping	32	●	●	●	●	●	●	●
Spreading with a table knife	Butter	32, 34			●	●	●	●	●
Scooping	Jacket potato		●	●	●	●	●	●	●

Skill	Ingredients for skill practice	Recipe numbers	4+	5+	6+	7+	8+	9+	10+
Mashing	Beans, potato, avocado	38, 39, 42, 59, 60, 68, 69		●	●	●	●	●	●
Crushing garlic	Garlic	38, 39, 41			●	●	●	●	●
Using a lemon squeezer	Lemon, lime, orange	21, 22, 27, 39, 40, 42, 43, 44, 59, 60, 68, 69	●	●	●	●	●	●	●
Mixing/beating ingredients together	Salad dressing, scrambled eggs	17, 20, 22, 23, 26, 27, 38, 39, 40, 41, 42, 43, 44, 52, 58, 59, 60, 69	●	●	●	●	●	●	●
Using a blender	Smoothie	58, 67					●	●	●
Whisking	Smoothies, egg whites, cream	26, 68		●	●	●	●	●	●
Shelling a hard boiled egg	Egg	24, 52				●	●	●	●
Garnishing and decorating	Herbs, paprika, cinnamon	21, 24, 27, 32, 42, 44, 52, 60	●	●	●	●	●	●	●
Seasoning to taste	Salt and pepper	39					●	●	●
Using a toaster	Bread	33					●	●	●
Using a rolling pin	Pastry, bread	34	●	●	●	●	●	●	●
Washing/draining through a sieve or colander	Lettuce, beans, vegetables	17, 20, 22, 23, 24, 26, 27, 33, 34, 38, 41, 42, 53, 55, 60, 67, 69		●	●	●	●	●	●

Equipment Checklist

Knife skills

- ☐ Chopping board
- ☐ Vegetable knife
- ☐ Kitchen scissors
- ☐ Grater
- ☐ Peeler

Weighing and measuring

- ☐ Measuring spoons, cups
- ☐ Measuring Jug
- ☐ Weighing Scales

Baking skills

- ☐ Rolling pin
- ☐ Baking trays/tins
- ☐ Blender
- ☐ Toaster

Other skills

- ☐ Table knife, fork, spoon
- ☐ Mixing bowl
- ☐ Potato masher
- ☐ Can opener
- ☐ Garlic press
- ☐ Kettle
- ☐ Glasses, plates, bowls (serving)
- ☐ Sieve/ Colander
- ☐ Whisk
- ☐ Lemon juicer
- ☐ Ladle
- ☐ Wooden spoon
- ☐ Spatula
- ☐ Cutters (biscuits, scones)

Food Safety at Home

Getting children involved in the kitchen is an invaluable skill for lifelong independence. Integrating food safety into that time will teach them how and why it's important to handle food safely and hygienically.

Preparation

- Wear a clean apron
- Wash your hands in warm soapy water before and after touching different foods
- Tie back long hair
- Ensure food surfaces and equipment are clean before use

Contamination

- Keep raw foods and cooked foods separate
- Use different chopping boards for raw or cooked foods
- Don't eat foods past their 'use-by' date
- Be allergy aware

Cooking/Creating

- Wash fruit and vegetables well before using
- Only take refrigerated ingredients out of the fridge before you need them
- Always return refrigerated items to the fridge after use
- Meat, fish, poultry and egg dishes need to be cooked to their recommended temperatures to destroy any bacteria

Cleaning

- Keep preparation surfaces clean
- Wipe up food spills immediately

Breakfasts

Bircher Muesli
Serves 4

Equipment

Tablespoon
Mixing spoon
Mixing bowl
Colander/sieve
Lemon juicer
Grater
Kitchen scissors/small knife
Weighing scales
Measuring jug

Ingredients

100g rolled oats
1 orange
1 tbsp. dried fruit
250ml milk (your choice)/apple juice
1 tbsp. mixed nuts
½ tsp. nutmeg/cinnamon
1 apple
2 tbsp. natural Greek yoghurt
Toppings - fresh berries, coconut

Method

1 Use kitchen scissors/small knife to chop the nuts and dried fruit into a bowl.
2 Squeeze the juice from the orange and add to the nuts and fruit.
3 Then add the oats, nutmeg/cinnamon and milk/apple juice, cover and leave in the fridge overnight.
4 For serving grate the apple and yoghurt and stir into the mix.
5 Spoon into your serving bowl and top with a topping of your choice.

(For serving – can sweeten with a tsp. of honey or maple syrup)

Nutrition know how

Oats are high in soluble fibre which means they are digested more slowly by the body helping us to feel fuller for longer and maintain even energy levels. They also contain a naturally calming compound which can help us feel more relaxed.

Dietary Adaptations

DF - soya/coconut yoghurt, alternative milk, **NF** - seeds

Coconut, Almond, Date & Apple
Serves 4

Equipment

Small knife for chopping

Chopping board

Mixing spoon

Mixing bowl

Blender

Measuring scales

Ingredients

40g dessicated coconut

40g flaked/ground almonds

20g soft dried dates

1 green apple

Method

1 Wash the apple and chop into chunks removing the core.

2 Place all the ingredients into blender and pulse until roughly combined.

3 Serve on its own or use as a fresh topping over yoghurt/muesli.

Nutrition know how

Dates are high in fibre and minerals such as potassium, magnesium, zinc and selenium linked to their immune boosting properties. Their soluble and insoluble fibre may help to calm stomach upsets and digestion.

Dietary Adaptations
NF - seeds

Choc Chia Pudding
Serves 4

Equipment

Teaspoon
Tablespoon
Mixing spoon
Mixing bowl
Measuring jug

Ingredients

2 tbsp. chia seeds
300ml milk (your choice)
2 tbsp. flaked almonds
2tbsp. goji berries/dried fruit
1tsp. cacao/cocoa powder

Method

1 Combine all the ingredients in a mixing bowl.
2 Stir well.
3 Cover and store in the fridge overnight.
4 Stir and before serving.

(For serving – if you prefer it to be sweeter add a tsp. of honey or maple syrup)

Nutrition know how

Chia seeds are rich in Omega-3 fatty acids, calcium, magnesium and fibre. They are thought to benefit our hearts, bones, teeth and digestion. When they are soaked a gel forms around the seed, so if you don't like the texture simply blend.

Dietary Adaptations
DF - Alternative milk - oat/coconut/rice/soya, **NF**- seeds

Make Your Own Muesli
Serves 4

Equipment

Small knife for chopping

Chopping board

Bowl for mixing

Bowl for serving

Dessert spoon

Container for storing

Tablespoon

Teaspoon

Ingredients

Choose different ingredients to create a unique recipe.

Choose from rolled oats, quinoa flakes, puffed brown rice, puffed millet, dried apple, soft dates, soft apricots, dried mango, dried banana, dried berries, coconut chips, sunflower seeds, linseeds, pumpkin seeds, poppy seeds.

Fresh milk and fruit for serving.

Method

1 Plan the different ingredients for your muesli.
2 Chop and prepare the different ingredients and combine together in a bowl.
3 Spoon into your container to keep fresh.
4 Try a portion with milk and add some fresh fruit (berries, bananas).

Nutrition know how

Dried fruit is high in sugar because the drying process removes the water content and the sugar becomes more concentrated. Eat dried fruit in moderation to provide natural sweetness.

Dietary Adaptations

DF - Alternative milk - oat/coconut/rice/soya, **NF**- seeds

Salads

Coleslaw
Serves 6

Equipment

Fork

Small knife for chopping

Grater

Jug

Chopping board

Bowl for mixing

Bowl for serving

Teaspoon

Tablespoon

Ingredients

3 tbsp. Greek natural yoghurt

½ tsp. Dijon mustard

1 tbsp. cider vinegar

½ small white cabbage

2 carrots

½ onion

Method

1 In the jug combine the yoghurt, mustard and vinegar stirring well.
2 Wash the carrots in running water.
3 Use the grater to grate the carrots and cabbage and put into your bowl.
4 Finely chop your onion and add to the bowl.
5 Pour the dressing onto the vegetables and mix well.
6 Spoon into your serving bowl to serve.

Nutrition know how

Cabbages are bitter foods, which help our bodies digest our food. They contain vitamin C, K and antioxidants that help to protect our skin and provide our liver with beneficial nutrients.

Dietary Adaptations
DF - soya yoghurt/mayonnaise

Couscous Salad
Serves 4

Equipment

Kettle (hot water)

Fork

Small knife for chopping

Jug

Small plate

Chopping board

Bowl for mixing

Bowl for serving

Teaspoon

Tablespoon

Weighing scales

Ingredients

100g couscous

200ml hot water

¼ tsp. Bouillon powder
(veg stock)

2 spring onions

1 red pepper

½ cucumber

50g feta cheese

2 tbsp. pesto

2 tbsp. pine nuts/mixed seeds

Method

1 Pour the water into the jug and stir in the bouillon.

2 Add the couscous to the hot water, stir and cover with the plate.

3 Finely slice the onion, pepper and add to mixing bowl.

4 Dice the cucumber and add to the bowl.

5 Check the couscous has absorbed all the water and use a fork to mix up.

6 Pour the couscous into the bowl, add the pesto and mix well.

7 Pour into the serving bowl and crumble over the feta.

8 Sprinkle the pine nuts on top and serve.

Nutrition know how

Sweet peppers are a member of the nightshade family, which includes tomatoes and potatoes. They contain vitamin C and antioxidants, which help to protect our eyes and our hearts.

Dietary Adaptations
DF - swap feta for dairy free cheese/chicken/tuna

© The Food Teacher

Greek Salad
Serves 6

Equipment

Small knife for chopping
Chopping board
Bowl for mixing
Bowl for serving
Lemon juicer
Tablespoon
Teaspoon
Weighing scales

Ingredients

4 large tomatoes
1 red onion
¼ cucumber
6 tbsp. olive oil
1 lemon
200g feta cheese
20 black olives

Method

1 Remove the core of the tomatoes and cut the flesh into chunks. Add to the bowl.
2 Slice up the red onion and add to the tomatoes.
3 Cut the cucumber into chunks and add.
4 Cut the feta into chunks and add to the bowl.
5 Next add the olives and mix carefully.
6 Squeeze the lemon and put the juice into the jug.
7 Add the olive oil to the jug and mix well.
8 Pour the liquid over the salad and spoon into the serving dish to serve.

Nutrition know how

Onions contain sulphur compounds, which give them antibacterial properties. They also contain prebiotics, which help to feed the healthy bacteria in our digestive tract.

Dietary Adaptations

DF - swap feta for dairy free cheese/chicken/tuna

Jewelled Rice/Pasta Salad
Serves 4-8

Equipment

Teaspoon
Tablespoon
Mixing spoon
Kitchen scissors
Mixing bowl
Bowl for serving
Colander/sieve
Chopping board
Weighing scales

Ingredients

150g cold cooked rice/pasta
½ green pepper
½ orange pepper
4 dried apricots
100g tinned red kidney beans
Small bunch of fresh coriander
2 tbsp. olive oil

Method

1 Put the rice/pasta into the mixing bowl.
2 Use the scissors to cut the peppers and apricots into small pieces.
3 Add to the rice.
4 Open the tins of beans and pour into the colander/sieve (over the sink).
5 Rinse and drain the beans and add to the rice.
6 Cut up the coriander with the scissors and sprinkle into the bowl.
7 Pour the olive oil over the rice and mix thoroughly together.

Nutrition know how

Rice is a staple food for around half the world's population. It's a great source of B vitamins and fibre. Opt for brown rice which has undergone minimal processing and is therefore richer in nutrients. Brown rice can support healthy cholesterol, provide energy, help to balance hormones and protect the digestive system. Keep cooked rice in the fridge to reduce any risk of food poisoning.

© The Food Teacher

Layered Rainbow Salad
Serves 4

Equipment

Small knife for chopping

Chopping board

Glass bowl for serving

Tablespoon

Sieve/colander

Ingredients

Choose different ingredients for layering thinking about colours.

Choose from red (peppers, tomato, radishes, red onion), orange (peppers, carrots), yellow (pepper, hard boiled eggs, sweetcorn), green (peas, cucumber, lettuce, pepper, avocado) and black (olives).

Method

1 Plan the different layers of your salad.
2 Chop and prepare each vegetable layer, then add to your serving bowl.
3 Once all your layers are added you can serve.

Nutrition know how

A rainbow of vegetables every day is beneficial because we increase our intake of naturally occurring plant chemicals (phytonutrients), which give the foods their colours. Benefits include keeping our eyes and skin healthy and supporting us to fight germs and infections.

Nutty Quinoa Salad
Serves 4

Equipment

Tablespoon
Small knife for chopping
Chopping board
Mixing spoon
Mixing bowl
Colander/sieve
Lemon juicer
Grater
Measuring scales
Bowl for serving

Ingredients

250g cooked quinoa
1 carrot
2 spring onions
40g beansprouts
25g cashew nuts
1tbsp. tamari/soy sauce
2tbsp. sesame oil

Method

1 Wash the carrot, beansprouts and spring onions in the colander/sieve and drain.
2 Grate the carrot and finely chop the spring onions.
3 Combine all the ingredients in the mixing bowl and mix thoroughly.
4 Spoon into your serving bowl.

(For serving – this salad tastes great with the Prawn Summer Rolls)

Nutrition know how

Quinoa is a good source of complete protein as it contains all the essential amino acids. So it's great for growing and helping the body repair. It also contains Omega-3 fatty acids and antioxidants so beneficial for our brain health too.

Dietary Adaptations

GF - Tamari sauce, **NF** - Seeds

© The Food Teacher

Three Bean Salad
Serves 4-8

Equipment

Teaspoon
Tablespoon
Mixing spoon
Whisk
Mixing bowl
Colander/sieve
Bowl for serving

Ingredients

1 tin (400g) cannelini beans
1 tin (400g) red kidney beans
1 tin (400g) black beans

For the dressing:
1 tsp. mustard
2 tbsp. balsamic vinegar
6 tbsp. olive oil

Method

1 Put the mustard, vinegar and olive oil into the mixing bowl and
   whisk together.
2 Open the tins of beans and pour into the colander/sieve (over the sink).
3 Rinse and drain the beans.
4 Pour the beans into the mixing bowl with the dressing.
5 Mix thoroughly.
6 Spoon into your serving bowl.

Nutrition know how

Kidney, black and cannellini beans
are all known as legumes and
grow from plants. They are a good
source of iron, which is important
for our red blood cells that carry
oxygen around our bodies.
This helps us to grow and gives
us lots of energy.

Tomato and Prawn Lettuce Wraps
Serves 6-8

Equipment

Teaspoon
Tablespoon
Mixing spoon
Mixing bowl
Colander/sieve
Lemon juicer
Plate for serving
Kitchen paper
Weighing scales

Ingredients

2 little gem lettuces
220g (8oz.) cooked peeled prawns

For the dressing:
½ lemon or lime
3 tbsp. natural Greek yoghurt
2 tsp. tomato purée
½ tsp. paprika

Method

1 Separate the lettuce leaves and put into your colander/sieve.
2 Wash in cold water.
3 Pat dry with the kitchen paper and lay out on the serving plate.
4 Now wash your prawns in the colander and pat dry.
5 Lay 3 or 4 prawns on each lettuce leaf.

Make the dressing
1 Squeeze the lemon or lime into the mixing bowl.
2 Add the yoghurt and tomato purée.
3 Stir together until you have a pink dressing.
4 Add 2 tsps. of dressing to each lettuce leaf.
5 Sprinkle the paprika on top to finish.

Nutrition know how

Prawns are a good source of protein rich in carotenoids, such as astaxanthin which gives prawns their pink colour. This is an antioxidant that can support immune function, brain health and may protect the eyes from damage. Prawns are also high in anti-inflammatory omega-3's.

Dietary Adaptations
DF - soya yoghurt/mayonnaise

© The Food Teacher

Sandwiches & Wraps

Finger Sandwiches
Serves 4-8

Equipment

Knife for spreading

Small knife for chopping

Chopping board

Biscuit cutters

Plate for serving

Ingredients

8 slices of bread

Butter/dairy-free spread

Sandwich fillings (cream cheese, sliced cheese, ham, hummus, tuna, cucumber, smoked salmon, lettuce)

Decoration – chives, cress

Method

1 Spread some butter onto one slice of bread.

2 Choose your filling and spread/layer over the butter.

3 Add the other slice on top and use a knife/cutters to cut into fingers, triangles, squares or shapes.

4 Decorate with paper flags, chives or cress.

Nutrition know how

Foods like meat, fish, cheese and hummus are rich in protein, which is needed for the body to grow and repair. It also helps to keep our concentration and energy levels even throughout the day so we need to think about eating protein with every meal.

Dietary Adaptations

GF - gluten free bread

Pitta Pockets
Serves 4

Equipment

Knife

Small knife for chopping

Chopping board

Bowl for mixing

Plate for serving

Tablespoon

Teaspoon

Toaster

Ingredients

4 wholemeal pitta breads

Fillings (cream cheese, cheese, ham, hummus, tuna, smoked salmon, cucumber, grated carrot, tomato, lettuce)

Method

1 Cut the pitta bread into 2 pockets and lightly toast until opened.

2 Fill the pitta pocket with a filling of your choice.

3 Place on your serving plate to serve.

Nutrition know how

When creating sandwiches it's important to consider the rainbow of vegetables which will accompany our protein source. These rainbow of colours will provide the body with a whole host of benefits and so are vital to plan for.

Dietary Adaptations

GF - gluten free pitta bread (don't use the same toaster)

Spiral Sandwiches/Wraps
Serves 4

Equipment

Knife

Rolling pin

Small knife for chopping

Chopping board

Plate for serving

Tablespoon

Teaspoon

Ingredients

8 slices of bread/wraps

Butter/dairy–free spread

Sandwich fillings (cream cheese, sliced cheese, ham, hummus, tuna, smoked salmon, cucumber, grated carrot, lettuce)

Method

1 If using bread, roll a rolling pin over each slice a few times. Use a sharp knife to cut off the crusts.

2 Spread each piece with butter and add a thick layer of filling.

3 Roll up each slice/wrap into a sausage shape and cut into smaller pieces.

4 Put onto a plate to serve.

Nutrition know how

Wraps can provide a great alternative to bread and can be made from a whole host of different foods to suit individuals, such as corn flour, iceberg lettuce, nori sheets or rice flour.

Dietary Adaptations

GF - gluten free wraps/iceberg lettuce leaves for wraps

Prawn Summer Rolls
Serves 4

Equipment

Mixing bowl

Small knife for chopping

Chopping board

Colander/sieve

Peeler

Plate

Sieve/colander

Method

1 Wash the mint leaves, carrot and spring onions.

2 Peel the carrot. Cut the carrot and spring onions into thin sticks (julienne).

3 Add lukewarm water to the mixing bowl (enough to dip the rice pancakes).

4 Dip one pancake into the water and leave for 20 seconds pull out and lay on the plate. Towards the bottom of the wrap fill a small rectangle with a mint leaf, 3 prawns, 2/3 carrots and spring onions and a few beansprouts. Roll from the bottom folding over the sides as you go to form a spring roll.

5 Repeat step 4 for the additional pancakes and serve with dipping sauce.

Ingredients

8 Spring roll wrappers (Rice pancakes)

24 fresh prawns (ready to eat)

8 large mint leaves

1 carrot

2 spring onions

Large handful of beansprouts

Dipping - Tamari/soy/sweet chilli sauce

Nutrition know how

Mint leaves provide lots of flavour and contain antiseptic and antibacterial properties, which make mint ideal for soothing upset stomachs and helping digestion. It can also help to balance the body to either energise or relax.

© The Food Teacher

Dips

Chunky Hummus
Serves 4

Equipment

Fork
Potato masher
Small knife for chopping
Chopping board
Garlic press
Colander/sieve
Jug
Lemon juicer
Bowl for mixing
Bowl for serving
Teaspoon
Tablespoon

Ingredients

1 tin (400g) chickpeas
2 tsp. lemon juice
1 garlic clove
1 tsp. ground cumin
3 tbsp. tahini
Water
2 tbsp. olive oil
1 tsp. paprika

Method

1 Empty the chickpeas into the sieve/colander and rinse under
running water.
2 Use the fork/masher to crush the chickpeas into a mash.
3 Peel the garlic and crush in the press. Add to bowl.
4 Squeeze the lemon and add the juice.
5 Add the tahini, olive oil and cumin.
6 Mix well and slowly add tbsp. of water to create a creamy
chunky texture.
7 Spoon into the serving bowl and sprinkle with the paprika to serve.

*(For serving – you could include rice crackers, oat cakes, carrot, cucumber,
celery sticks)*

Nutrition know how

Chickpeas are legumes and grow
from plants. They are a good
source of iron, which is important
for our red blood cells that carry
oxygen around our bodies.
This helps provide energy, helps
us to grow and repair the body.

Guacamole
Serves 4

Equipment

Fork

Small knife for chopping

Garlic press

Chopping board

Bowl for mixing

Jug

Lemon juicer

Bowl for serving

Teaspoon

Ingredients

2 ripe avocados

2 cloves of garlic

Lime

1 red onion

¼ red chili

1 large vine tomato

2 tbsp. fresh/frozen coriander

Black pepper

Method

1 Cut the avocado in half, squeeze slightly to remove the stone and squeeze all the flesh out of the skin into the mixing bowl.

2 Mash the avocado with a fork.

3 Squeeze the lime and add the juice to the avocado and mix well.

4 Finely chop the onion and add to bowl.

5 Finely chop the chilli and add to bowl.

6 Chop the tomato into small chunks and add to bowl.

7 Peel the garlic and crush in your crusher. Add to bowl.

8 Finely chop your coriander and add to bowl.

9 Stir the ingredients together and spoon into a serving bowl to serve.

Nutrition know how

Avocados are rich in vitamins and minerals and contain twice as much potassium as a banana. This is great for keeping blood pressure even. Avocados are also full of beneficial monounsaturated fats, great for brain health.

© The Food Teacher

Mackerel Pâté
Serves 4

Equipment

Teaspoon
Tablespoon
Mixing spoon
Fork
Mixing bowl
Colander/sieve
Lemon juicer
Bowl for serving
Kitchen scissors

Ingredients

1 mackerel fillet (tin)
½ lemon or lime
12 fresh chives
2 tbsp. sour cream

Method

1 Squeeze the lemon/lime to remove the juice.
2 Flake the mackerel using a fork into the mixing bowl (**check for bones**).
3 Cut the chives using the scissors.
4 Mix the chives, lemon/lime juice and cream with the mackerel.
5 Mix thoroughly.
6 Spoon into your serving bowl.

(For serving – you could include rice crackers, oat cakes, carrot, cucumber, celery sticks)

Nutrition know how

Mackerel is an oily fish, which is high in omega-3 fatty acids. These are important for our brain to work and grow as these fats provide us with lots of energy. Omega-3 fatty acids may help our brain with learning and memory.

Dietary Adaptations
DF - soya yoghurt/mayonnaise

Paprika Dip
Serves 4

Equipment

Knife
Small knife for chopping
Chopping board
Garlic press
Bowl for mixing
Bowl for serving
Tablespoon
Teaspoon
Weighing scales

Ingredients

300g cream cheese
1 tsp. tomato purée
2 tbsp. natural Greek yoghurt
2 spring onions
1 garlic clove
2 tsps. paprika

Method

1 Put the cream cheese in a bowl and add the tomato purée and 1 tbsp. of the yoghurt. Mix well then add the rest of the yoghurt. Mix again.
2 Slice the spring onions into small pieces and add to the bowl.
3 Crush the garlic and add the paprika. Stir well.
4 Spoon into the serving bowl to serve.

(For serving – you could include rice crackers, oat cakes, carrot, cucumber, celery sticks)

Nutrition know how

Natural yoghurt contains 'healthy' bacteria, which live in our digestive tract and help with our absorption of food. These bacteria also help to strengthen our immune system helping us to fight germs.

Dietary Adaptations

DF - soya yoghurt/mayonnaise/dairy free cream cheese

Smashed Bean Dip
Serves 6-8

Equipment

Teaspoon
Tablespoon
Mixing spoon
Fork
Potato masher
Mixing bowl
Colander/sieve
Lemon juicer
Bowl for serving

Ingredients

1 tin (400g) cannellini beans
1 tin (400g) chickpeas

For the dressing:
½ lemon
4 tbsp. natural Greek yoghurt
2 tsp. cumin
1 tsp. olive oil
1 tsp. mixed seeds

Method

1 Open the tin of beans and chickpeas.
2 Put into colander/sieve and rinse under water and drain.
3 Pour into the mixing bowl and crush with a fork and/or masher.

Make the dressing
1 Squeeze the lemon into the mixing bowl with the beans and peas.
2 Add the yoghurt, oil and cumin.
3 Mix well.
4 Spoon into the serving bowl and sprinkle the mixed seeds on top to finish.

(For serving – you could include rice crackers, carrot or celery)

Nutrition know how

Olive oil is rich in fat soluble vitamins D, E and K. It contains more monosaturated fats than any other natural oil. For its nutritional benefits it is best consumed cold as a dressing or in dips. It can help to protect against heart disease and support digestion.

Dietary Adaptations

DF - soya yoghurt/mayonnaise

Sour Cream and Chive Dip
Serves 4

Equipment

Kitchen scissors
Cup
Jug
Bowl for mixing
Bowl for serving
Tablespoon
Teaspoon
Chopping board
Small knife for cutting
Weighing scale

Ingredients

25g fresh chives
300 ml sour cream
1 tsp. lemon juice
Carrot and cucumber for dipping

Method

1 Put the chives in a cup and use the kitchen scissors to chop into tiny pieces.
2 Save 1 tbsp. of chives in the cup and add the rest to the mixing bowl.
3 Squeeze the lemon and add the juice to the bowl.
4 Pour the sour cream into the bowl and mix well.
5 Spoon into the serving bowl and top with the saved chives.
6 Cut up some carrot and cucumber sticks for serving.

(For serving – you could include rice crackers, oat cakes, carrot, cucumber, celery sticks)

Nutrition know how

Culinary herbs, such as rosemary and chives provide flavour in our food and also have a host of healthful properties. They can have antibacterial effects and help our digestion. The choline they contain can also support sleep, learning and memory.

Dietary Adaptations

DF - soya yoghurt/mayonnaise

Tuna Dip
Serves 6-8

Equipment

Teaspoon
Tablespoon
Mixing spoon
Mixing bowl
Colander/sieve
Lemon juicer
Plate for serving
Kitchen paper

Ingredients

1 tin (160g) tuna

For the dressing:
½ lemon
3 tbsp. natural Greek yoghurt
½ tsp. mustard
½ tsp. paprika
Decoration - chives

Method

1 Open the tin of tuna and drain away any liquid.
2 Put the tuna into a mixing bowl and use the fork to break it into flakes.

Make the dressing
1 Squeeze the lemon into the mixing bowl with the tuna.
2 Add the yoghurt and mustard.
3 Mix well.
4 Spoon into the serving bowl and sprinkle the paprika on top to finish.
5 Decorate with chives
(For serving – you could include oat cakes, carrot or celery)

Nutrition know how

Tuna is an oily fish, which is high in omega-3 fatty acids. These are important for our brain to work and grow as these fats provide us with lots of energy.
Omega-3 fatty acids may help our brain with learning and memory.

Dietary Adaptations
DF - soya yoghurt/mayonnaise

Yoghurt and Mint Dip
Serves 4

Equipment

Teaspoon

Mixing spoon

Mixing bowl

Small knife for chopping

Chopping board

Colander/sieve

Lemon juicer

Weighing scales

Bowl for serving

Ingredients

150g natural Greek yoghurt

¼ cucumber

1 tsp. lemon juice

5 mint leaves

Method

1 Wash the cucumber in the sieve/colander and drain. Finely chop the cucumber and add to the mixing bowl.

2 Use the juicer to squeeze the lemon and add 1 tsp. to the bowl.

3 Finely chop the mint leaves and add to the bowl.

4 Add in th yoghurt and combine well.

5 Spoon into your serving bowl.

(For serving – you could include rice crackers, oat cakes, carrot, celery sticks)

Nutrition know how

Lemons are from the citrus fruit family and contain high levels of vitamin C. They are also rich in antibacterial compounds and can support our digestive health. When added to foods they also help to preserve the colours and flavours.

Dietary Adaptations

DF - soya yoghurt/mayonnaise

© The Food Teacher

Snacks

Apple Slices
Serves 4

Equipment

Teaspoon
Tablespoon
Colander/sieve
Small knife for chopping
Chopping board
Table knife for spreading
Plate for serving

Ingredients

4 apples
4 tbsp. peanut/cashew/almond/
seed butter
3 tbsp. rolled oats
1 tbsp. dried fruit

Method

1 Wash the apples in the sieve/colander and drain well.
2 Slice off the stalk of the apple and cut large slices in the same direction.
3 Lay the slices on the chopping board and cut out the core from the centre of some of the pieces.
4 Top each slice with peanut/seed butter, and sprinkle with oats and dried fruit.
5 Place all your slices on a plate and serve.

Nutrition know how

Nut butters such as cashew and almond are a good source of protein and contain high levels of antioxidants which help our immune system, eyes, joints, circulation, brain and growth.

Dietary Adaptations
NF - seed butter

Celery Boats
Serves 4

Equipment

Small knife for chopping
Chopping board
Teaspoon
Tablespoon
Table knife for spreading
Colander/sieve
Plate for serving

Ingredients

3 celery sticks
2 slices of smoked salmon
2 tbsp. cream cheese
½ lemon

Method

1 Wash the celery in the sieve/colander and drain.
2 Cut each celery stick into 4 pieces (boats).
3 Fill each boat with cream cheese and top with smoked salmon.
4 Gently squeeze the lemon over the boats.
5 Place on the plate for serving.

(Alternatives – you could include parma ham, chicken pieces, hummus)

Nutrition know how

Salmon is an oily fish, which is high in omega-3 fatty acids. These are important for our brain to work and grow as these fats provide us with lots of energy. Omega-3 fatty acids may help our brain with learning and memory.

Dietary Adaptations

DF - dairy free cream cheese/cashew nut cream

© The Food Teacher

Egg Mayonnaise Spiders
Serves 4

Equipment

Fork

Small knife for chopping

Chopping board

Bowl for mixing

Plate for serving

Tablespoon

Teaspoon

Ingredients

4 hard-boiled eggs

2 tbsp. natural Greek yogurt

12 pitted black olives

Method

1 Peel the hard boiled eggs.

2 Cut in half and scoop the yellow yolk into the bowl.

3 Use the fork to mash the egg yellows and add the yoghurt stirring well.

4 Cut the olives in half keeping 8 for the spider body.

5 Cut the other halves into 4 spider legs each.

6 Spoon the egg mayonnaise mixture into the egg whites.

7 Then decorate with the olives to create your spiders.

8 Place onto your serving plate to serve.

Nutrition know how

Eggs are a source of good quality protein. They also contain vitamin D, which is important for our bones and teeth. Egg yolks contain antioxidants which help to protect our eyes and they are also a great source of choline, B vitamins and fats that provide fuel to our brains helping us to learn and remember.

Dietary Adaptations

DF - soya yoghurt/mayonnaise, **Egg Free** - use mini oat cakes, dairy free cream cheese and olives

Fruit Kebabs
Serves 4

Equipment

4 kebab sticks

Small knife for chopping

Chopping board

Plate for serving

Colander/sieve

Ingredients

Raspberries

Strawberries

Grapes

Blueberries

Method

1 Wash your berries and grapes in the colander/sieve.

2 Cut your strawberries in half.

3 Thread your ingredients onto the kebab sticks, alternating colours.

Nutrition know how

Berries contain lots of antioxidants, which are like 'superheroes' in our bodies helping to keep us fit and healthy. They tend to be found in lots of brightly coloured foods and help support digestion and keep the eyes and brain healthy.

Dietary Adaptations

If allergic to strawberries choose grapes instead

© The Food Teacher

Instant Berry Jam
Serves 4

Equipment

Teaspoon
Tablespoon
Mixing spoon
Small knife for cutting
Chopping board
Fork
Mixing bowl
Colander/sieve
Jar for serving/storing
Weighing scales

Ingredients

150g fresh strawberries
2 tbsp. chia seeds
1/2 tsp. honey/maple syrup
to sweeten

Method

1 Wash the strawberries in the sieve/colander and drain well.
2 Remove the top of the strawberries and cut into quarters and place in the bowl.
3 Then use the fork to mash the strawberries to a pulp.
4 Mix in the chia seeds and the sweetener.
5 Pour into a jar and leave for at least 1 hour to set firm.

(For serving – you could include rice crackers, oat cakes)

Nutrition know how

Strawberries are high in vitamin C, which supports our immune system, teeth, bones and gums. They also support heart and digestive health and are most nutritious when eaten whilst in season, during the summer months.

Dietary Adaptations

If allergic to strawberries use other berries/apple purée

Veggie Kebabs
Serves 4

Equipment

4 kebab sticks

Small knife for chopping

Chopping board

Plate for serving

Colander/sieve

Ingredients

Mozzarella pearls

8 cherry tomatoes

¼ cucumber

8 pitted olives/black grapes

Fresh basil leaves

Iceberg lettuce –for displaying
the kebabs (optional)

Method

1 Wash your cucumber and tomatoes in the colander/sieve.

2 Chop your cucumber into slices.

3 Thread your ingredients onto the kebab sticks, alternating colours.

4 Put the pointed end into the lettuce at the end for display.

Nutrition know how

Tomatoes are actually a fruit. They are rich in vitamin C and a plant chemical called lycopene, which gives them their bright red colour. Lycopene has been known to protect the eyes, skin and support the body to fight germs and infections.

Dietary Adaptations

DF - dairy free hard cheese, cubed

Desserts

Apricot Seed Bars
Serves 12

Equipment

Small knife for chopping
Chopping board
Square baking tin
Parchment paper
Tablespoon
Teaspoon
Blender
Hob/microwave
Container for storage
Weighing scales

Ingredients

120g coconut oil/butter,
room temperature
200g mixed seeds
(sunflower, pumpkin)
60g jumbo oats
30g ground flaxseeds
250g soft, dried apricots, chopped
1 orange

Method

1 Melt the coconut oil/butter if necessary, otherwise stir till soft.
2 Blend the oats and seeds to form a flour.
3 Grate the orange and add the zest to the bowl.
4 Add the other ingredients into the blender and pulse until mix resembles breadcrumbs.
5 Stir in the melted coconut oil/butter.
6 Press into a square tin lined with parchment paper.
7 Chill in the fridge for at least an hour.
8 Remove and cut into bars and store in the fridge.

Nutrition know how

Apricots are rich in fibre and vitamins A, C and E, ideal for digestive health, eyes and skin.

Avocado and Lime Mousse
Serves 4

Equipment

Small knife for chopping

Fork

Chopping board

Bowl for mixing

Bowl for serving

Tablespoon

Grater

Lemon juicer

Teaspoon

Ingredients

2 ripe avocados

3 limes

1 tsp. vanilla extract

2 tbsp. honey/maple syrup

Method

1 Cut the avocado in half, squeeze slightly to remove the stone and squeeze all the flesh out of the skin into the mixing bowl.

2 Use the fork to mash until smooth.

3 Grate the limes removing the zest.

4 Cut the limes in half and squeeze out the juice.

5 Add the zest, juice, vanilla extract and honey to the bowl and mix well.

6 Pour into a bowl to serve.

Nutrition know how

Honey is a natural sweetener which contains dextrose and fructose sugars. As it is natural it also contains vitamins and minerals, which provide other benefits to our bodies.

© The Food Teacher

Avocado Orange Chocolate Mousse
Serves 4

Equipment

Fork

Small knife for chopping

Chopping board

Mixing bowl

Tablespoon

Lemon juicer

Grater

Bowls/ramekins for serving

Ingredients

2 ripe avocados

2 tbsp. cacao/cocoa

2 tbsp. honey/maple syrup

1 orange

Zest/Dark chocolate chunks for
decoration (optional)

Method

1 Cut the avocado in half, squeeze slightly to remove the stone.

2 Squeeze all the flesh out of the skin into the mixing bowl.

3 Mash the avocado until smooth.

4 Squeeze the juice of the orange and add to the avocado.

5 Mix in the cocoa and honey and stir well.

6 Spoon into bowls and decorate with the zest/chocolate chunks.

Nutrition know how

Maple syrup is a natural sweetener with energy boosting properties. It contains minerals and properties which are anti-bacterial and rich in antioxidants, that can support heart health. Look for 100% maple syrup and avoid those with added sugars.

Coco Choc Mousse
Serves 6

Equipment

Teaspoon
Tablespoon
Mixing spoon
Grater
Bowls/ramekins for serving
Blender

Ingredients

400ml full fat coconut milk
3tbsp. cacao/cocoa powder
1tsp. vanilla extract/paste
125g soft dried dates

Topping - dark chocolate/dessicated coconut/fresh raspberries

Method

1 Put the coconut milk in the fridge over night.
2 Place all the ingredients into a blender and pulse until smooth.
3 Divide between 6 bowls/ramekins and store in the fridge before serving.
4 Top with dark chocolate/dessicated coconut or fresh raspberries.

Nutrition know how

Coconut is a fruit. The milk is the juice from the white flesh and this is high in medium-chain triglycerides, which are healthy fats that can support our heart health, balance our appetite and feed our brains.

Lemon Bliss Balls
Serves 8

Equipment

Grater

Plate for serving

Weighing scales

Blender

Ingredients

100g of soft dried dates

200g ground almonds/mixed seeds

100g dessicated coconut

1 lemon

50g chia seeds

1 tbsp. honey/maple syrup (optional)

Method

1 Grate the lemon to remove the zest and add the zest to a blender.

2 Add all the other ingredients to the blender and pulse until well combined.

3 Roll mix into teaspoon sized balls and store in the fridge before serving.

Nutrition know how

Almonds are a good source of the minerals zinc and magnesium. They are also rich in vitamin E, which supports our immunity, brain, heart and skin health. They are also rich in fibre so they can help to keep our blood sugars even.

Dietary Adaptations

NF - seeds

Traffic Light Sorbet
Serves 4

Equipment

Blender
Tablespoon
Bowls for serving
Weighing scales

Ingredients

3 chopped, frozen bananas
10g spinach
100g frozen strawberries
100g frozen mango pieces

Method

1 Add one banana and the spinach to a blender and pulse until combined and creamy. Add to the bottom of the serving bowls.
2 Add the next banana and the mango and pulse. Then add as the next layer to the serving bowl.
3 Finally pulse the strawberries and the last banana and add to the top of the bowls.
4 Eat immediately or cover and freeze for later.

Nutrition know how

Mangoes are high in vitamin C boosting our immune system, protecting our eyes and skin . They also contain enzymes which help to break down protein and fibre keeping our digestive system healthy.

Drinks

Blueberry Banana Smoothie
Serves 4

Equipment

Tablespoon
Jug/measuring cup
Blender
Colander/sieve

Ingredients

1 banana
2 cups liquid - coconut water/water/
apple juice
2 cups blueberries (fresh/frozen)
1 tbsp. mixed seeds
2 tbsp. Greek natural yogurt/dairy
free alternative

Method

1 If using fresh blueberries wash them in the colander/sieve and drain.
2 Place all the ingredients into the blender.
3 Blend together
4 Pour into glasses/cups to serve.

Nutrition know how

Bananas are rich in potassium, which helps us to absorb other nutrients such as calcium so beneficial for our bone health. They also provide us with sugars such as quick release glucose and slower release fructose providing us with an energy boost.

Dietary Adaptations

DF - soya/coconut yoghurt

Green Smoothie
Serves 4

Equipment

Small knife for chopping
Chopping board
Jug/measuring cup
Blender

Ingredients

2 cups spinach/kale
2 cups liquid – water/coconut
water/coconut milk/almond milk
3 cups fruit (mixture) – banana/
mango/berries/avocado/
peach/grapes

Method

1 Wash your green leaves in the colander/sieve and drain.
2 Place into the blender with your chosen liquid.
3 Blend together.
4 Prepare and chop your chosen fruit and add to the green liquid.
5 Blend again until smooth.
6 Pour into glasses/cups to serve.

Nutrition know how

Spinach and kale both contain vitamin K, which helps to strengthen our bones. They also contain calcium and iron, which can be easily absorbed by the body from these foods.

© The Food Teacher

Pineapple Smoothie
Serves 4

Equipment

Fork

Small knife for chopping

Chopping board

Bowl for mixing

Jug

Lemon juicer

Glasses/cups for serving

Teaspoon

Ingredients

2 small bananas

1 lime

1 tsp. runny honey

150g natural Greek yoghurt

½ pint (300ml) pineapple juice

Method

1 Peel the bananas and put them into the mixing bowl.

2 Use the fork to mash them until smooth and pour into the jug.

3 Cut the lime in half, squeeze out the juice and add the juice to the jug.

4 Put in the honey and mix well.

5 Add the yoghurt and pineapple juice and use the fork to whisk until frothy.

6 Pour into glasses/cups to serve and drink **immediately**.

Nutrition know how

Pineapples contain vitamin C and an enzyme called bromelain, which helps our digestion and to repair the body if we get injured. It also helps us to fight off germs and infections especially sore throats.

Dietary Adaptations

DF - soya/coconut yoghurt

Raspberry Punch
Serves 4

Equipment

Small knife for chopping

Potato masher

Chopping board

Lemon juicer

Colander/sieve

Mixing bowl

Glasses/cups for serving

Ingredients

4 oranges

1 small punnet of raspberries

330ml still/sparkling water

Method

1 Cut the oranges in half and juice them.

2 Pour the juice into the 4 glasses/cups.

3 Wash the raspberries in the colander/sieve and put them in the mixing bowl.

4 Mash the raspberries until them become a pulp.

5 Spoon the pulp into the 4 glasses/cups.

6 Slowly top up with the water.

Nutrition know how

Oranges are rich in vitamin C and may support the heart, the immune system and kidney health. Vitamin C rich foods also support the absorption of iron, which is especially important for growing children and women.

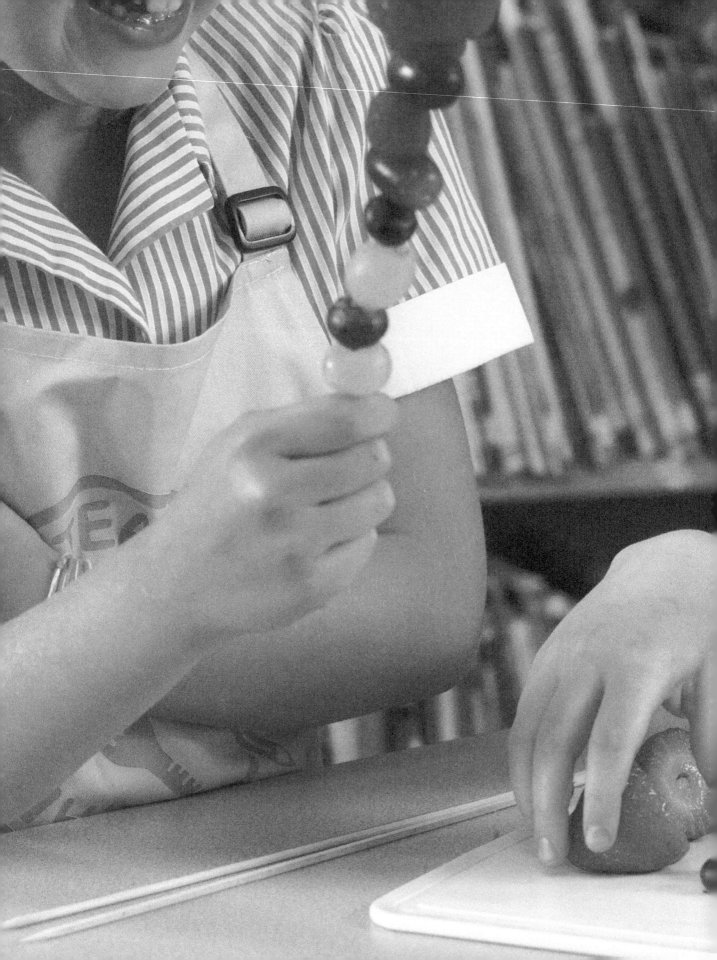

Nutrition Know How

Macronutrients

Nutrient	Food Sources	Recipes	Function
Fats	Meat, fish, dairy foods, coconut, avocado, nuts and seeds, olive oil	14, 15, 16, 17, 22, 25, 27, 32, 33, 34, 35, 38, 39, 40, 41, 43, 44, 45, 50, 51, 52, 54, 55, 58, 59, 60, 61, 62, 66, 68	A good balance of polyunsaturated, monosaturated and saturated is needed for optimal health, brain and nerve function, energy and metabolism. Helps us to absorb fat soluble vitamins A, D E and K.
Protein	Meat, dairy, legumes (beans, chickpeas), wholegrains, nuts and seeds	14, 15, 16, 17, 20, 21, 22, 23, 25, 26, 27, 32, 33, 34, 35, 38, 39, 40, 41, 42, 43, 44, 45, 50, 51, 52, 54, 55, 58, 59, 60, 62, 66, 68	Needed for growth and repair of body tissues and for hormones and enzymes.
Carbohydrates	Wholegrains (rice, pasta, bread), oats, potatoes, legumes, cereal	14, 17, 21, 23, 25, 26, 32, 33, 34, 35, 38, 42, 58, 62	Good source of energy. Healthier choice is to choose complex carbohydrates rather then white, processed grains.
Fibre	Wholegrains, legumes, fruit and vegetables, nuts and seeds	14, 15, 16, 17, 20, 21, 23, 24, 25, 26, 32, 33, 34, 38, 50, 51, 53, 54, 55, 58, 61, 66, 67, 68	Important for digestive health, lowers cholesterol and regulates appetite.

Macronutrients — Vitamins

B Vitamins (Water soluble – so sources best steamed or raw)

Nutrient	Food Sources	Recipes	Function
Vitamin A (Fat soluble)	Liver, carrots, apricots, dark green leafy vegetables, fish	17, 20, 21, 23, 24, 27, 32, 33, 34, 35, 44, 58, 67	Antioxidant, which quenches damaging free radicals. Beneficial for sight, growth and repair, bones and teeth.
B1 – Thiamin B2 – Riboflavin B3 – Niacin B5 – Pantothenic Acid B6 – Pyridoxine B9 – Folic Acid	Yeast extract (Marmite), liver, fish (tuna), meat, nuts and seeds, wholegrains, avocado	14, 15, 16, 17, 27, 32, 33, 34, 35, 40, 44, 50, 54, 58, 59, 60, 62	Use fats and protein to release energy. Important for cell growth, nervous system, hormones and digestion.
Vitamin B12 – Cobalamin	Liver, shellfish, oily fish, eggs, meat, dairy	20, 27, 32, 33, 34, 35, 40, 41, 43, 44, 45, 51, 52, 55, 66, 68	Used for cell formation including red blood cells, therefore important for healthy nervous system, blood cells, digestive system and skin. Deficiency linked to anaemia (low red blood cells, pale skin, low energy). Plants do not contain bioactive forms – imp. for vegans to supplement/ fortified foods, e.g. Marmite
Vitamin C	Rainbow of fruit and vegetables: dark green leafy vegetables, sweet peppers, berries	17, 20, 21, 22, 23, 24, 25, 27, 32, 33, 34, 39, 53, 54, 55, 63, 66, 67, 68, 69	Antioxidant supporting healthy immune system, wound healing, bones, teeth and gums. Supports absorption of iron. High temperatures can reduce levels.
Vitamin D	Oily fish, seeds, dairy, mushrooms, fortified foods (cereals)	14, 17, 20, 22, 25, 27, 35, 40, 44, 50, 52, 55, 58, 62, 66, 68	Needed for calcium absorption, therefore important for bones and teeth, healthy immunity, nervous system support and hormone balance.
Vitamin E	Nuts and seeds, oils (olive), wholegrains, avocados, tomatoes, broccoli	14, 15, 16, 17, 21, 22, 24, 25, 27, 32, 33, 34, 39, 54, 55, 58, 59, 60, 62	Antioxidants supporting healthy immune system, skin, tissue healing, circulation, hormones, fertility and growth.
Vitamin K	Dark green leafy vegetables, turnip, oats, legumes	KS1: 18, 22, 26, 28 KS2: 46, 50, 58, 60, 62, 66, 68	Needed for energy, bone health, blood sugar balance, skin and immunity.

© The Food Teacher

Major Minerals

These minerals are required by the body in larger quantities.

Nutrient	Food Sources	Recipes	Function
Calcium	Seaweed, dairy, dark green leafy vegetables, legumes, broccoli, almonds	14, 15, 17, 20, 21, 24, 26, 27, 32, 22, 34, 35, 38, 40, 41, 42, 43, 44, 45, 52, 55, 58, 62, 63, 66, 67, 68	Most abundant mineral in body. For bones and teeth, hormones, nerves and muscles and blood pressure.
Phosphorus	Nuts and seeds, cheese, chicken, eggs, lentils	32, 33, 34, 52, 55, 51, 58, 62	Needed to support healthy bones, and energy production.
Potassium Sodium Chloride	Nuts and seeds, spinach, mushrooms, broccoli, banana, red meat	15, 17, 24, 25, 32, 33, 34, 38, 50, 51, 54, 58, 62, 63, 66, 67	All electrolytes – mineral salts that conduct electricity when dissolved in water. Regulate blood pressure, water balance, hormone, muscle and nerve health.
Sulphur	Eggs, legumes, wholegrains, garlic, onions, brussel sprouts, cabbage	17, 20, 21, 22, 23, 24, 26, 32, 33, 34, 38, 39, 42, 43, 52, 67	Needed for protein structure such as joints, hair, nails and skin.
Magnesium	Kelp, seaweed, nuts and seeds, spinach, apricots, dates, avocado	15, 16, 17, 22, 25, 27, 35, 38, 39, 50, 58, 59, 60, 61, 62, 63, 67	Important for bone strength, nerve and muscle function. Also needed for tissue repair and energy production.

Trace Minerals

Nutrient	Food Sources	Recipes	Function
Chromium	Liver, beef, wholegrains, potatoes	14, 17, 21, 23, 32, 33, 34, 58, 62	Supports blood sugar balance and cholesterol regulation.
Copper	Nuts, butter, legumes	14, 15, 17, 21, 25, 26, 32, 33, 34, 38, 42, 58	Needed for iron absorption, red blood cells, skin, bones and nerves.

Nutrient	Food Sources	Recipes	Function
Iodine	Seaweed, shellfish, dark green leafy vegetables	14, 21, 22, 23, 24, 32, 33, 34, 35, 60, 67	For metabolism and optimal function of thyroid gland and production of hormones.
Iron	Clams, molasses, nuts and seeds, liver	15, 21, 22, 23, 24, 25, 27, 32, 33, 34, 58, 67	Needed for red blood cell function, energy release and growth. Also important for healthy skin and nails. Vitamin C enhances absorption.
Manganese	Nuts, spinach, oats, avocado	15, 16, 17, 50, 54, 58, 59, 60, 62, 63, 67	Antioxidant important for bone formation and brain health.
Selenium	Oats, tuna, garlic, eggs	14, 17, 25, 20, 38, 39, 44, 50, 52, 58, 62	Antioxidant that works with vitamin E. Important for reproduction, thyroid health and body repair.
Zinc	Oysters, ginger, red meat, nuts and seeds, legumes	17, 21, 25, 26, 32, 33, 34, 38, 42, 54, 58, 62	Antioxidant and immune system regulator. Important for wound healing, skin, hair and muscle health and growth.

Other Nutrients

Nutrient	Food Sources	Recipes	Function
Essential fatty Acids – Omega Oils	Oily fish, milk, oils (linseed, walnut, hempseed)	14, 15, 16, 17, 22, 25, 27, 32, 33, 34, 35, 39, 40, 44, 50, 54, 58, 59, 60, 62	Important to regulate inflammation, growth, brain function, nervous system, eyes, skin, circulation, heart, hormone and joint health.
Phytonutrients – Plant chemicals – e.g. quercitin, rutin	Rainbow of fruit and vegetables	20, 21, 22, 23, 24, 27, 32, 33, 34, 35, 39, 53, 55, 58, 59, 60, 63, 66, 67, 68, 69	Antioxidants supporting healthy immunity, growth, repair, brain function, nervous system, circulation, eyes, skin, joints, metabolism and hormones.

© The Food Teacher

Glossary

Beat	To mix ingredients together using a fast, circular movement with a fork, spoon or whisk
Blend	To mix ingredients together gently using a fork or spoon
Breadcrumbs	Finely grated or ground mixture made from bread
Bridge Knife Cut	To make a bridge with the thumb and index finger and holding the knife under the bridge cut downwards
Claw Knife Cut	To shape your fingers into a claw, which rests on the food and as the food is sliced the claw slowly moves away from the knife
Chill	To cool down an ingredient or a dish by placing in the fridge
Chop	To cut into small pieces
Chunks	To cut into large pieces
Combine	To mix together
Core	The central part of the food, which contains the seeds
Crush	To squeeze something very hard to break it into smaller parts
Cut	To make something smaller using scissors or a knife
Decorate	To make something look more interesting before serving
Dice	To cut into small cubes
Drain	To remove the liquid
Equipment	The tools that are needed for a particular recipe
Flake	To break up an ingredient into smaller, thin pieces
Garnish	To decorate food before serving
Grate	To scrape food against the holes of a grater to make smaller pieces
Ingredients	The foods which are used in a recipe to create a dish
Juice	The liquid that can be squeezed out of fruit and vegetables
Julienne	To cut food into long, thin strips

Line	Cover a baking tray/tin with paper or butter so food doesn't stick to it
Mash	To squash food with a fork, masher or spoon
Melt	To slowly heat a food to turn it into a liquid
Mix	To stir ingredients together with a fork or spoon
Peel	To remove the skin of a fruit or vegetable
Pour	To tip one food into a bowl or onto other foods
Press	To push or squeeze something firmly
Pulp	A soft, wet mixture made when food is mashed/pressed
Pulse	Short, fast blends or beating of a mixture
Recipe	The instructions for how to prepare a food/dish
Rinse	To use water to clean off a food
Roll	To make something smooth and flat using a rolling pin
Season	To improve the flavour of a food by adding herbs or spices
Serve	To prepare food or drinks ready to be eaten
Separate	To divide up ingredients, e.g. separate the egg yolk from the white
Scoop	To dig out a substance to put somewhere else
Slice	To cut off a thin, piece of food from a larger piece
Snip	To cut something with scissors
Spread	To use a knife to cover something with a softer food, e.g. to cover a piece of bread with butter
Sprinkle	To drop a few pieces of food on the top of a dish
Squeeze	To press something firmly to remove the liquid
Stir	To mix ingredients together using a circular movement using a fork, spoon or whisk
Tear	To pull/break something apart using your fingers
Thread	To push foods onto a stick
Toast	To warm a food up by putting it near heat
Wash	To clean a food off in water
Whisk	To beat foods together to add air and make the food lighter
Zest	Skin of an orange, lemon or lime, which can be used to add flavour to food

© The Food Teacher

How The Food Teacher Can Help You

The Food Teacher provides FREE resources for families providing health advice, competitions and recipes (mostly gluten-free) including some amazing guest recipes.

The Food Teacher Clinic offers 1:1 nutritional consultations for individuals and/or families taking them through a 4-step approach to change.

The Food Teacher clinic also works with individual children and their families through schools to improve nutrition to reduce obesity risk, improve concentration, attendance (boosting immunity), support reluctant eaters, behaviour and support children with special educational needs.

Sign up and contact **The Food Teacher** to discuss your needs further.

www.thefoodteacher.co.uk
www.facebook.com/thefoodteacheruk
Email: info@thefoodteacher.co.uk

Lightning Source UK Ltd.
Milton Keynes UK
UKOW07f0739181115

262985UK00001B/4/P